Express Yourself

Use art to explore the emotions inside you!

by
Emma MacLaren Henke

★ American Girl®

Dear Reader,

Are you ready for an exciting kind of art book that explores what you're feeling as you create? That explores the choices you make? That explores *how* you do something rather than how well you do it?

Your goal in *Express Yourself* won't be to create a picture-perfect piece of art. Instead, you'll create art to see what you can learn about yourself, your family, your friends, and your community.

Express Yourself will also show you that art is often ignited by emotions. Your feelings guide your ideas, your inspiration, and your approach to art. Creating art helps you work through your feelings and understand them more clearly. And art allows you to make emotional connections with other people and the world around you.

Are you ready to learn what your art reveals about you? The projects in this book will help you find out—and you're sure to have fun along the way!

Your Friends at American Girl

How to Use This Book

The projects in this book are for you. Don't worry if you think you're not a great artist. Just focus on what making art teaches you about yourself and your feelings.

You can work straight through the book or jump from project to project. Many of the art assignments are great to share with your friends. Get together, and get creative!

Before you begin your projects, ask an adult to help you choose a well-protected work surface—especially when working with paints.

Most of the projects in this book use supplies you may already have on hand. Collect the following materials, and you'll be ready to begin almost any of them!

- Pens, pencils, markers, and crayons
- Watercolor paints
- Nontoxic acrylic paints
- Paintbrushes
- Plain notebook paper

- Construction paper
- Poster board
- Scissors
- Craft glue
- Tape

Art Journal

"Express Yourself" questions will appear after most of the projects. To get the most from this book, do the art projects BEFORE YOU READ the journal questions. Then use the journaling pages to explore what each activity meant to you.

Drawing Out Your Feelings

This chapter isn't about creating art to hang on your walls. Instead, you'll explore the things that inspire you to make art in the first place. Maybe you'll collect pictures of puppies because they make you happy, or purple objects because they remind you of a close friend, or soft things because they make you feel safe. And you can gather more than images and objects—if words inspire you, pull those out, too!

Inspiration Station

Create a special space for all your best art ideas.

You will need:

- A large cork bulletin board
- Pushpins
- Tape

Make a collection of art starters. Search for pictures, objects, and words that stir your imagination, and attach them to the bulletin board. Your collection will make it easier to find inspiration when you need it.

Ask an adult if you can cut out inspiration from old magazines, catalogues, and newspapers. Collect pictures, words, or symbols that strike you as beautiful or startling or stylish—anything that suggests a particular emotion to you. Does a photo of a hot-air balloon make you feel free? Clip it out. Does a serious news headline make you feel curious? That's perfect for your board, too.

Next, look through your own photos for inspiration. Choose family pictures that make you feel happy or excited or loved. They'll help you conjure up those feelings later on. Be sure to ask your parents if it's OK to attach the photos to the board, or make photocopies to use instead.

Then, check your closet and drawers for small personal items that you can add to your board. Maybe a favorite hair ribbon makes you feel confident, or a fuzzy sock makes you feel comforted.

Check your recent school projects, too. Do you have something you're really proud of? Pin it up.

Look for paper or fabric color blocks that inspire you. Or make lists of your art ideas, and place them on the board.

Allow your board to evolve. Continue to add things to it or remove things that no longer inspire. It's just for you! When you're stuck for an art idea, check out your board.

7

An Artist's Touch

Professional artists and crafters often use inspiration or mood boards. Before they begin a project, they might dedicate a board to a particular color, theme, or feeling. Take a look at these inspiration boards to get an idea of how one might look. What images inspire you most?

I ♥ horses!

Tip: Look at your own board. Think about how it makes you feel.

Stack Your Deck

Draw, doodle, and color to create a deck of emotions cards.

You will need:

- Unlined index cards
- Pens, pencils, markers, and crayons

Do you ever have a hard time figuring out just how you feel? This project may help you understand what different emotions mean for you.

To begin, write the name of a different emotion on each note card. You might want to start with some of these feelings, but add your own emotion words, too:

happy afraid embarrassed interested overwhelmed elated excited angry frustrated ashamed bored lucky lonely nervous proud stressed-out content shy sad loving hopeful jealous grateful sorry worried pleased ambitious anxious brave thrilled hopeless silly

On the back of each note card, create a quick sketch or doodle to represent what that feeling or emotion means to you. Or if you prefer, cut out a picture of that emotion, and glue or tape it to the card. Don't think too long about what you want to draw or show, and don't spend more than a few minutes on each card. Your images can show people and things, or they can show patterns, designs, or even scribbles.

There's no need to make the deck all at once, and you can add cards to your deck whenever you like.

The next time you can't pin down exactly what you're feeling, flip through the art on your cards. Which words and pictures best show your mood? Later on, as you work on some of the other projects in this book, you might find that you have a hard time expressing how you feel. When you get stuck, remember to check your deck.

Tip: As the days, weeks, and months pass, you might find a picture that better reflects how you feel, or you might even change your idea about what that emotion means to you. If that happens, simply update your deck. Redo cards to allow your emotions to grow with you!

Find Your Feelings

How do you feel right now? Sometimes it's hard to say, right? But the projects on the next pages will show you how to record your emotions using art. You'll also see how creating different kinds of art can help you explore and experience different emotions.

Doodle Diary

Keep track of your feelings through sketches and scribbles.

You already know how to keep a journal: make an entry each day to record what happened or what's on your mind. But did you ever think of adding doodles to your diary? What would happen if you used drawings, rather than writing, as the main way to get your thoughts down on the page? Give it a try!

Here are a few tips to help you begin:

- Fill the pages of a notebook with your ideas. Your sketches can be illustrations of your exact thoughts or things that happen to you, but they can also be patterns or scribbles that represent your thoughts.

- Don't feel as if you have to draw only what happened to you or what you're thinking about. You can also draw or sketch whatever you feel like creating at that moment.

- Jot down a few words to describe each drawing, and add the date, too. Then, when you look back on the diary weeks or even years from now, it'll mean more to you.

- Remember, doodling and sketching can be great ways to relax. Don't judge what you create—just try to get something down on paper.

Tip: If you find, after doodling for a few days, that you love keeping a doodle diary, look for a special journal or sketchbook to continue your work!

Stretch a Sketch

Take a look at your doodles. They could say oodles about you!

What do the pages of your doodle diary look like? Are they sprinkled with stars or filled with flowers? Do you color in the open spaces in your letters or fill the margins with looping scribbles?

Take this fun quiz, and see if you discover a little more about your personality. Use a few pages from your doodle diary as your sample to answer these questions. Or grab a sheet of paper and spend ten minutes drawing random doodles and scribbles to use instead.

1. When you doodle, do you usually
  a. start at the left and work to the right?
  b. start at the right and work to the left?

What it means:
  a. You're a dreamer—creative and sensitive.
  b. You're a thinker—logical and practical.

2. Which does your doodle look more like?

a. b.

What it means:
  a. Dark, heavy strokes can mean that you're having a hard day.
  b. Light strokes? You're in a great mood!

3. Where is your doodle?
  a. left side of the page
  b. right side of the page
  c. top of the page
  d. center of the page
  e. bottom of the page

What it means:
  a. You're quiet and reserved.
  b. You're sociable and optimistic.
  c. You're enthusiastic!
  d. You like to be the center of attention.
  e. You're reluctant to push yourself.

4. Which scribble did you do?

   a. fill in or decorate letters

   b. draw complicated patterns

   c. write your name over and over

   d. draw a wandering line

What it means:

   a. You're a good team player.

   b. You're a shy girl.

   c. You're figuring out who you are.

   d. You're distracted.

5. Which shapes show up most in your doodles?

   a.   b.   c.

What it means:

   a. You're brainy.

   b. You're decisive.

   c. You're levelheaded.

6. Which of these doodles did you draw?

   a.   b.   c.

   d.   e.

   f.   g.

What it means:

   a. You're gentle and nice.

   b. You're optimistic and energetic.

   c. You're a daydreamer—very imaginative.

   d. You're protective of your friends.

   e. You're ambitious and always ready for action.

   f. You're full of hope.

   g. You're cheerful and happy.

Doodle Decoder

Take a closer look at what your doodles might reveal about you.

You're flexible.

You're feeling intense and determined.

You're ambitious. You want to move up in the world.

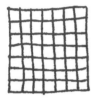

Do you feel trapped?

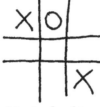

You're looking for a challenge.

Do you feel strong love for someone?

You're feeling positive.

Look at the expressions on the faces you've drawn to reveal how you're feeling.

Tip: Some experts believe that doodling relaxes your brain and can help you be more creative. The next time you're having trouble with a project, don't be afraid to doodle away. You never know what you might discover.

Project Yourself

Self-portraits can show how you really see yourself, and they can also show others who you are as a person.

Animal Instinct

"Paws" to play with your wild side.

Close your eyes and picture yourself slowly becoming an animal. Which parts of your personality would translate into animal form? Would you love to fly? Are you happy spending time by yourself? Do you like to run free? Do you like to play in snow, or would you choose to sleep through winter?

Now open your eyes, and sketch yourself as an animal below. Or, if you want to paint your animal, sketch it here first and then paint it on a piece of watercolor paper or canvas. Think about the trait you like best in the animal you chose, and title your work with that trait.

Out of the Picture

Have an out-of-body experience!

If you drew a self-portrait, what would it include? Would you show your eyes and hair? How about your body, or even your feet? What if you drew yourself without showing any part of your actual body? Could you do it?

Some artists draw self-portraits using only triangles, scribbles, or images that represent who they are, such as eyeglasses, a paint-brush, a pattern, or shadows.

Get a sheet of paper, and create a portrait of yourself that does not show your body. You can draw, color, or make a collage—whatever feels most comfortable for you. If you want to paint your idea, use watercolor paper or canvas.

Mirror, Mirror

When you look in a mirror, who (or rather, what!) is looking back?

Draw a self-portrait that highlights what you love most about yourself—but turn your portrait into an object. Say, for example, you love that you're a great reader. You could draw yourself as a book wearing your favorite outfit!

Now, draw an object that features the things you dislike about yourself. For example, if you don't like that you snore, you could draw a giant nose perched on your bed pillow!

Wonder Woman

You have the power to play!

Draw yourself as a superhero below. Make sure to describe or show your super-powers. Include some super-tools that might help you breeze through a tough experience, such as a funeral, a fight with a friend, or a difficult test.

23

On the Other Hand
Part 1

Give yourself a hand for trying this project.

One of the best reasons to try something new (out of all of the really great reasons to try something new) is that you don't have to be perfect. You can explore! And isn't this one of the reasons you love art in the first place?

So, try this. Draw something below—anything—using your non-dominant hand. That is, if you're right-handed, draw with your left hand, and if you're left-handed, use your right hand. Work as quickly or as slowly as you like.

On the Other Hand
Part 2

Return to your comfort zone.

Now draw exactly the same picture, but use your dominant hand.

Picture Imperfect

A picture is worth a thousand words.

Create a collage at right made up of things that you **don't** want to be a part of your life. Think about the items you select for your collage. Your portrait can include silly choices, such as taco-flavored pickles, or serious ones, such as rude attitudes. Fill your portrait with images and words from magazines, too. Let your collage dry before turning the page.

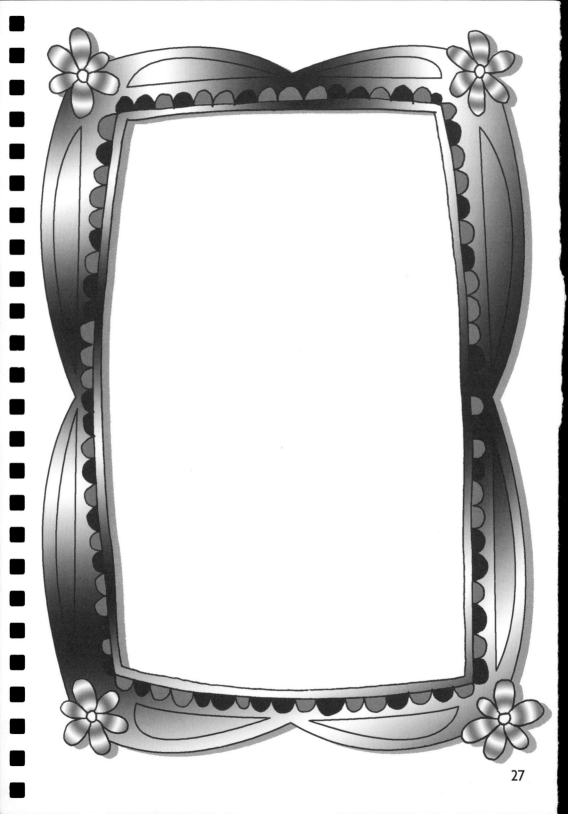

Shape-Shifter

Try your hand at this activity.

Without looking at your hand, use a crayon to draw a life-size outline of your hand below. Then place your hand on the page. Using a different color, trace your hand over the outline you drew. Was the hand a different size? Bigger or smaller?

Now, using chalk on the sidewalk or a crayon on a big sheet of butcher paper, draw a life-size outline of what you think is the shape of your body. Ask a family member or friend to trace the actual outline of your body over your first drawing.

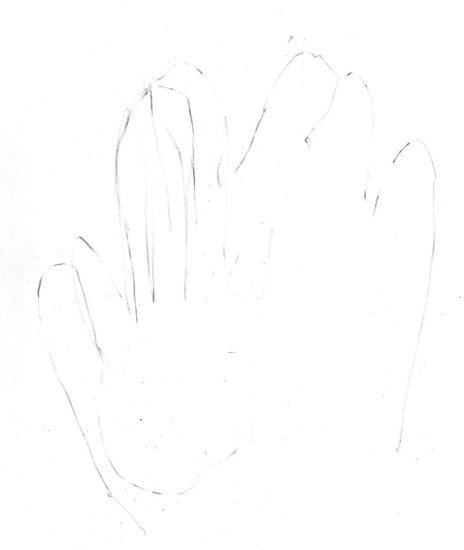

Logo Show

Design a symbol to show how you feel about yourself.

Logos are small works of art that make us think of the group or product they stand for. Design a logo below that represents you! You might start with a simple shape or image that you like, such as a star or a heart or a balloon. Then add details that show your feelings or personality traits. Try out different colors and textures you like. When you're done, show your logo to friends or family and ask them if they think the logo fits your personality.

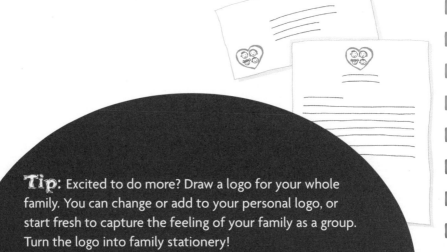

Tip: Excited to do more? Draw a logo for your whole family. You can change or add to your personal logo, or start fresh to capture the feeling of your family as a group. Turn the logo into family stationery!

Textures and Tints

Does your fuzzy pink robe make you feel warm and happy? Would a scratchy gray sweater ruin your day? The colors you see and the textures you touch can affect your emotions and your choices. The projects on the next few pages will help you explore how color and texture stir up certain feelings.

Color Love

What does your favorite color say about you? See if you agree with the personality traits shown below.

Red
Your boldness and energy help you go after your goals.

Orange
You're enthusiastic and friendly.

Yellow
You're creative, and you look on the bright side.

Green
You're smart, and you care about your community.

Blue
You're responsible and trusting, and you like to help others get along.

Purple
You're independent and generous.

Pink
You're warm, nurturing, and refined.

True Colors

Take this quiz to find out how much you know about the stories colors tell. Turn the page for the answers.

1. This color, known to stir feelings of passion and anger, actually makes your heart beat faster when you see it.
   a. blue   **b. purple**   **c. red**

2. Naturally, the human eye can tell the difference between more variations of this color than any other.
   a. green   **b. blue**   **c. red**

3. Warning! Don't dress in these two colors together unless you want to signal "Danger Ahead."
   a. blue and orange   **b.** yellow **and black**   **c. purple and** pink

4. In America, more people choose this calming color as their favorite than any other.
   a. purple   **b.** green   **c.** blue

5. Since this fun color is known to make people feel hungry, you'll often see it on food packages and restaurant signs.
   a. green   **b.** orange   **c. purple**

6. This color, historically worn by kings and queens, suggests mystery. Perhaps that's because it's made up of two colors that have opposite meanings: excitement and calm.
   a. purple   **b.** orange   **c.** green

7. This powerful color makes people think of elegance and class but also fear and death.
   a. red   **b. black**   **c.** white

Answers

1. **c. red**—Scientists have proven that people's heart rates and blood pressure go up when they see red.

2. **a. green**—You'll find many shades of green in nature, from forest green to sage to lime.

3. **b. yellow** and **black**—In nature, yellow and black signal danger: just think of bees. The human eye notices yellow better than most colors, so yellow and black work well to get people's attention on school buses and warning signs.

4. **c. blue**—Blue makes people feel calm, actually lowering heart rate and blood pressure. Blue also suggests quality—think of blue ribbons!

5. **b. orange**—Orange makes you hungry and grabs your eye, too—perfect for food companies trying to sell you snacks!

6. **a. purple**—Purple is made by mixing hot, bold red and soothing, cool blue.

7. **b. black**—Black is a popular color for clothing today, but in the past people mainly wore black to show that they were mourning the death of a loved one.

Hands On

Get messy and find out that finger painting is not just for preschoolers!

You will need:

• A covered work area to protect against paint spills

• A large sheet of finger-paint paper or poster board

• Finger paints or thick, nontoxic craft paints

When you paint with your fingers, it's easy to mix colors on the page. Experiment with blending the shades most pleasing to you. Create several new colors.

Using the paints you have mixed and a clean sheet of paper, paint a picture. If you're not sure what to paint, try making a picture with individual fingerprints. Or put down a thick layer of color with your fingers, and then use your fingernails to scratch patterns and designs in the paint. Or make a random smear of several colors on half of the paper, and then fold the paper in half over the paint. Open the page to see what image you've created.

Against the Grain

Make a textured grid to explore your feelings in 3-D.

Shape and color aren't the only ways to express your emotions through art. The texture or feel of the supplies you work with can bring out different emotions, too. Collect supplies from around the house. You can gather samples of things you've worked with before, or try some of the supplies on this list:

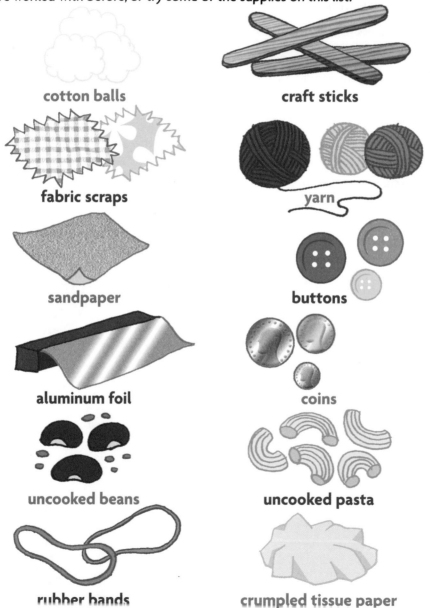

cotton balls

craft sticks

fabric scraps

yarn

sandpaper

buttons

aluminum foil

coins

uncooked beans

uncooked pasta

rubber bands

crumpled tissue paper

Draw a simple grid on poster board. Then, using Glue Dots® or craft glue, attach each item to a separate square on your board.

Now take some time to touch the textures of the items you've collected. Do any of the spaces in the grid bring out a particular feeling? Perhaps scraps of flannel make you feel warm and safe, or maybe the cool smoothness of foil or coins makes you feel calm.

Label your texture grid with the emotions the different supplies suggest to you.

Keep in Touch

Turn your favorite textures into a piece of 3-D art.

Choose textures you like best from the grid on the previous page, and use items with those textures to create a larger collage or picture on poster board.

Paint with Feeling

If you enjoy creating art with texture, try mixing your own 3-D paint.

In a small bowl, stir 2 tablespoons of nontoxic acrylic paint or finger paint with 1 tablespoon of any of these add-ins:

- Uncooked rice
- Glitter
- Uncooked cornmeal
- Sugar or salt
- Seed beads
- Sesame or poppy seeds

Use your textured paint to add depth to any project.

Mood Magic

Expressing emotions through art
can improve your mood and attitude,
but did you know that it can also
improve the mood of others who see
your work? Use the projects in this
chapter to deal with your emotions,
no matter what your mood.

Scribble It Out

Part 1

Feeling angry? This project lets you scribble away your troubles.

Sometimes, when you're mad, you can feel better if you express your emotions in a physical way. Start by gathering a stack of paper thick enough to pad your work surface so that your scribbles won't damage it. Then make a hard scribble on the top blank sheet of paper. Scribble on more sheets of paper if you're really feeling angry. Your lines and shapes can go in any direction and have any form you choose. Try to actually press your feelings out through your pencil. Set your scribble aside for half an hour or so, and then read the next page.

Scribble It Out

Part 2

Feeling calmer? Now make something constructive from your scribble.

Look at a scribble. Does it (or one of your other scribbles) look like anything specific to you? Choose one scribble, and use it as the start of a new drawing. You can draw about whatever made you angry, or you can draw something that the shape of your scribble suggests to you. If you like, add color to your picture with markers or crayons. Or draw designs in the spaces around your scribble to create a vivid image.

Heart Art

Create a collage inside a heart to show what you love.

You will need:

- Poster board or a large sheet of paper
- Pens, pencils, markers, and crayons
- Paints and paintbrushes
- Copies of photos
- Scissors
- Glue
- Old magazines

Draw a large heart on your poster board or paper. Now fill the heart with images of things you love. Create a collage of people, pets, special moments—anything that makes your heart soar. Thinking about what you want to include in your collage before searching for images will help make your heart art very special.

If you want to use photos of family or friends, be sure to get permission first or make photocopies. You can also draw portraits of your pets or cut out pictures of the music or books you enjoy. Sketch a favorite memory or two. It's up to you!

Tip: If you like, cut out your heart art when you're done filling it in. Keep it as a giant valentine to yourself. You can also make another heart for someone special as a way to share your love.

Pocket Vacation

Turn a candy tin into a relaxing getaway! Then, the next time you're stressed, take a vacation in your mind.

You will need:

- Empty mint or candy tins
- Small photos of yourself
- Pictures from travel magazines or brochures
- Stickers
- Glue
- Small souvenirs

Create a scene from the vacation of your dreams by decorating a candy tin inside and out.

✳ Add a photo of yourself next to cutouts from travel magazines.

✳ Include scrapbooking cutouts and rhinestones to add sparkle to your scene.

✳ Use adhesive foam pieces to make a cutout 3-D. Put foam between two copies of the same photo for a fun effect.

✳ Use glue to attach seashells or other small souvenirs to your tin.

✳ Don't forget to decorate the lid.

This is a great project to share with a friend—you can help her when she needs an escape, too!

Shifting Sands

Create patterns and pictures in a personal zen garden as a way to clear your mind.

You will need:

- A gift box or shirt box, 8" x 10" or larger
- Sand
- A fork
- Natural objects such as small stones, sticks, and shells

A *zen garden,* or Japanese rock garden, is a dry garden made of neatly raked sand, stones, and other natural objects. Taking care of a zen garden can help free your mind from distractions. As you tend your garden, concentrate on the sensations and physical actions that you're doing in this moment. Try not to think about what you have to do later or what happened yesterday. You might find that the feel of the sand soothes you. Or perhaps the repetition of raking will free your mind from stressful thoughts.

To make your indoor zen garden, fill the box with a layer of sand about ¼ inch deep. Use the sandbox like a sketchpad and doodle with your finger. When you want to create a new image, just give your box a shake to level the sand and begin again. Get used to the feel of the sand on your fingers.

Next, use a fork to make wave or swirl patterns in the sand. Create a pattern that feels tranquil to you. To add dimension to your garden, position natural items on the sand in pleasing places. Keep your zen box on your desk so that it'll be nearby anytime you're studying or stressed or you just need to clear your mind. Keep children, pets, and your garden safe by putting the top on the box when you're not using it.

A Perfect Painting

Feeling down? Paint a picture of your perfect day
to cheer yourself up.

You will need:

• A large sheet of paper or poster board

• Watercolor or nontoxic acrylic paints

• Paintbrushes

Spend a few minutes remembering one of the best days you've ever had. Maybe
your favorite day was when you got a new puppy. Or perhaps you remember
a birthday you spent with your whole family.

Next, think about how you would plan your own perfect day. Would you win the
school spelling bee, have a horseback-riding lesson after school, and eat dinner
at your favorite restaurant? Would you hike with your family in the mountains
and cook s'mores before snuggling into your sleeping bag? You decide.

Choose a scene from your best day ever—or imagine the perfect day—and
paint it. Try not to critique yourself as you paint—just go with the flow. Are
other people involved in your scene? Show them your painting when you're
done. They'll love knowing they're a part of your special day.

Dream Drawing

Doodle from a dream to discover what it might mean.

Keep a notepad and pencil by your bed for several nights. If you wake up and remember having a dream, write a few notes right away about what happened in your dream.

Choose one of your dreams to turn into a picture. Draw one scene from a dream, or show everything that happened in the dream with a series of sketches. You can even create a comic book to depict your dream. As you draw, focus on what you remember from your dream. Use your notes.

Keep your finished drawing with your notes.

Confidence Boost

Illustrate your greatest traits!

Paying attention to the things you love about yourself can improve your mood and give you confidence.

Begin by writing your name in the middle of the page at right. Around your name, draw pictures of things that you're good at. Are you an ice-skater who also loves to sing? Draw some skates, and add a few musical notes. Include illustrations to show your favorite features and personality traits, too. Do you love your curly hair? Are you proud of your good grades? Add a sketch of your favorite hairstyle and a fancy "A+" to your page. Decorate your name with colors and symbols you like. Use stickers, ribbons, pictures cut from magazines, or anything else you choose.

Tip: Want to share a smile? Make this project for a friend to show her why she's fantastic!

Smiling Eyes

Turn your frown upside down with a pair of googly eyes and an animal photo.

You will need:

- Photos of your pet or another animal
- Googly eyes
- Glue Dots
- Adhesive paper or sticky notes

Sometimes, we all need a laugh. Use Glue Dots to attach googly eyes to a picture of your pet or another animal. Cut adhesive paper to make a speech balloon. Then think of something funny for the animal in the picture to say, and write it carefully in the balloon. Stick it on the pic to make your critter speak!

Fun or funny projects can improve your mood! Try the same technique with copied pictures of yourself and your friends. Show your funny photos to your pals to share a laugh with them. Think about other ways to use humor in your art.

Knead to Relax?

Creating with clay can release frustration and soothe your nerves. Give one of these projects a try when you're feeling tense or angry.

You will need:

- Modeling clay or play dough
- Household items (a fork, a comb, blunt-ended toothpicks, etc.) to shape the clay
- A clean, flat, covered work surface

On the work surface, start molding the clay with your hands. Stretch it, smash it, pinch it. You don't need to make anything specific—just knead or roll the clay with your hands to help yourself feel calm. Pay attention to how handling the clay makes you feel.

Next, use everyday items to add texture to the clay. Cut it with scissors, or rake it with an old comb or a fork. Use the objects and clay to create textures that are pleasing to you. If you like, create a tile that features a favorite pattern or texture. Just flatten the clay, cut it into a square or rectangle, add texture, and let the clay dry.

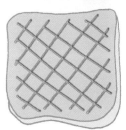

ROOOaaaRRR!

Godzilla

Spend a few minutes thinking about a situation that is making you angry or upset. Then use clay to form simple likenesses of people or things involved in that situation. Don't worry too much about details or how your figures look. Very rough models are fine.

Set up a scene with your clay creations. Then pretend you're Godzilla, and pound your clay figures flat. Try to express your anger or frustration as you pound. You can even growl or roar like Godzilla, too.

Drawing in the Dark

When you feel you're judging yourself or your art too harshly, turn out the lights.

Clear your work space, and pull out a large piece of paper and a pencil. Then turn out the lights. Draw a picture in the dark, without stopping to look at what you are drawing. Add as many details as you wish, but try to draw for at least two minutes. Then turn on the lights, and take a look at what you've created. Repeat as many times as you like.

Line Up

What can you draw with a single line?

This project has only one strict rule: draw an object without lifting your pen or pencil from the paper. Choose a simple object to draw—perhaps a pet, a car, or a tree. Following a specific rule can free you from your inner art critic. If you follow the rule, you give up control over the outcome of your project.

Before you start to draw, spend a moment picturing the object. Think about the shape and how its different parts fit together. Then try to imagine how the object will look when you draw it. When you have a clear picture in mind, start to draw. Remember, you must keep your pencil on the paper until your drawing is complete.

After you've completed one drawing, take a close look at it. What do you like in the drawing? What would you change? Try the drawing again, making the changes you had in mind.

Art Songs

Get in tune with your creativity by painting to music.

Painting to music helps you work without judging what you're creating. Listening to music can also help you paint in a free-flowing manner.

Collect paper, watercolor paints and brushes, and a variety of music. First, play music that makes you feel happy. Then start to paint. Let your paintbrush flow along to the music, painting whatever you like. Next, try painting to sad or slow music.

Later, choose one of your favorite songs, and play it on repeat. Try to capture what the song means to you in your painting. Remember to work freely. Just do what feels right. Your painting can be completely abstract, it can be a pattern, or it can show a scene the song brings to mind. You're in charge. Don't stop to correct yourself. Your painting is just for you.

Tip: Try this activity with a friend, too. Get together and paint to the same music. Don't peek at your friend's paper as she's working. When you're done, compare what you've created.

Share Your Feelings

So far, you've focused on making art to explore your own emotions. But art is also public. It's meant to be shared. Art can help you connect with people around you. Some of the projects on the next few pages let you work with friends. To learn even more about yourself, exchange feedback when working together. Other projects show you how to use art to make a connection with people in your community—to make a difference in their lives.

Bud Beads

Make a friendship bracelet more special by adding meaningful charms and a cute tag.

You will need:

- Elastic cord
- Colored beads
- Charms
- Colored paper
- Pens

Make a simple bracelet by stringing charms and colorful beads on a piece of elastic cord. Double-knot the ends, and clip off any long pieces. Choose colors and charms that show what your friend loves. If she's crazy about pink and adores dogs and stars, choose those for her gift. Attach a tag to explain what your bracelet means. That way, only you and your friend will know its secret.

Emily, I just wanted to paws long enough to tell you you're a special friend

Lexi, Here are the butterflies on a bracelet so that you won't have them in your stomach. Break a leg at the talent show!

Award Show

Celebrate your pals with ribbons that pay tribute to their greatest traits.

You will need:

- Construction paper
- Pens
- Glue
- Decorative ribbon
- Photos
- Stickers
- Sequins, beads, or other decorative craft supplies

Have you ever won an award? How did it make you feel? Would you like to share that feeling with all your friends?

Cut a shape, such as a star, out of colored construction paper. On that shape, write words describing an award that you'd like to give to a friend. Highlight what you love about her.

Glue strips of decorative ribbon to the back of the award. Embellish your awards with photos, stickers, sequins, or other decorative touches. Make ribbons for all your friends, and don't forget to make some for yourself, too!

Art for All

Use these art ideas to connect with your community!

Window Wonders

Paint a window to show your spirit or support a cause. Get permission from teachers or the principal to decorate a window at school. Or ask a local library or community center if you can decorate a window. Plan a painting that shares holiday cheer or helps to promote an upcoming event. Work with a group of friends to create your masterpiece. Make sure to use window paint or window markers, available in craft stores, so that your scene is easy to clean off the window—and when it's time for the decoration to come down, don't forget to return to do the cleanup job yourself.

Craft Sale

A craft sale is a great way to get creative with your friends and raise money for a good cause. To begin, choose a charity and let your customers know where you'll be donating. Next, find a place to set up your sale. Ask an adult to help you find out how to set up a table at a craft fair at a local community center or place of worship. Or hold a sale at your home, inviting friends, family, and neighbors. You can also check with your principal to see if you can sell crafts at school.

Decide what kinds of crafts you want to make and sell. Handmade greeting cards, friendship bracelets, and holiday decorations are great items for a sale. Set a time to meet with your friends and create the crafts you'll sell.

When the day of the sale arrives, display your products neatly, and try to price your items fairly. Charging at least twice as much as you spent for supplies to make each craft is a great place to start.

Remember to be safe. Make sure to ask an adult to help out on the day of your sale. Keep your cash out of sight in a safe place, too. When you're done, donate the profits to the charity you chose.

Supply Drive

Organize an art-supply drive to collect materials for a school in need or a local community center. Check with the art teacher at your school or the director of a local community center, kids' program, or senior center to find out if art supplies are needed. When you find a program in need, ask questions and make a detailed list of the supplies the program requires.

Then ask your principal if you can pass out flyers and collect art supplies at school. On the flyer, include your supply wish list. Use a laundry basket or plastic tub as the donation station for the supplies. Then give what you collect to the art program you're supporting.

Art Album

Collect drawings, paintings, and other two-dimensional artwork from your classmates. Ask a grown-up to help you scan the art into the computer. Then, using a photo website or a copy shop, work with an adult to make the art collection into a book you can sell to your classmates' parents. Donate the profit you earn to your school's art department or another good cause.

Co-op Collages

Begin a collage on friendship, and then let friends take over. Paste pictures, stickers, words, and other decorative items about friendship onto a piece of colorful poster board. Make sure to cover your work area, and leave plenty of space for friends to add to the collage. When you've finished with your portion, pass on the unfinished collage to a friend. That person can add to the collage and give it back to you or pass it on to someone else. When your collage is full, get together with all those who contributed to talk about what you've created. If you like, you can donate your collage to a children's hospital or a senior center.

How Did You Express Yourself?

While working through the projects in this book, you've learned how to pay attention to what's going on inside you when you create art. You've seen how art can be beautiful and touching even when your finished artwork is not what you expected. You know now that the experience of making art is just as important as the work of art you end up with when a project is done.

Perhaps you've learned to think about art in a new way. Art is a tool you can use to uncover what you're really feeling. Art helps you cope with tough times in your life. And through art, you can share the beauty of your happiest times.

You are worth sharing!

Express Yourself

1. Did you enjoy creating these projects?
2. Did you learn something about yourself?
3. Would you like to share this with us?

Write to:

Express Yourself Editor
American Girl
8400 Fairway Place
Middleton, WI 53562

(All comments and suggestions received by American Girl may be used without compensation or acknowledgment. We're sorry, but we can't return photos.)